CW01513016

Original title:

Whispers of Truth

Author: Swan Charm

ISBN HARDBACK: 978-1-80561-034-2

ISBN PAPERBACK: 978-1-80561-595-8

Ciphers of the Night

In shadows deep, the whispers dwell,
Silent echoes weave their spell.
Stars align in cryptic grace,
Guiding souls through time and space.

Hidden truths in darkness sigh,
Gentle winds that softly fly.
Dreamers chase the fading light,
Unraveling ciphers of the night.

A moonlit path, a secret dream,
Threads of fate, a silver seam.
Restless hearts in quiet dance,
Embrace the night, their only chance.

With each breath, a story told,
In silent realms where dreams unfold.
The mystery of night so bright,
Unveils the ciphers, pure delight.

In twilight's haze, our spirits roam,
Seeking solace, finding home.
In every glance, a world ignites,
As we decode the ciphers of the night.

Threads of Unraveled Secrets

In corners dark, where whispers weave,
The tapestry of truths believe.
Threads of gold, and shadows grey,
Unraveled secrets find their way.

With gentle hands, the fabric shows,
The hidden paths where wisdom flows.
Every stitch a quiet tale,
Of love, of loss, a whispered veil.

In silence kept, the echoes hum,
A symphony of what's to come.
Each secret spun, a tender thread,
Connecting hearts, where words have fled.

Amidst the chaos, stillness speaks,
In every silence, wisdom seeks.
Beneath the surface, stories lie,
In the threads of secrets, we rely.

As daylight fades, the night unfolds,
New tales emerge, their worth untold.
We trace the paths, explore the depths,
In threads of secrets, truth begets.

The Quietude of Awareness

In quiet spaces, the mind can roam,
Finding solace, a comforting home.
Thoughts like whispers, gently flow,
In peaceful silence, we come to know.

Awareness blooms in stillness rare,
A world beyond the rushing air.
In every heartbeat, a chance to see,
The quietude within you and me.

Moments linger, softly bright,
Echoing softly in the night.
With closed eyes, the spirit speaks,
In the quiet of awareness, the heart seeks.

Gentle breezes brush the skin,
Reminding us where we begin.
In each breath, a sacred space,
The quietude of life we embrace.

As dawn unfolds its golden rays,
We rise anew in gentle praise.
In subtle whispers, magic sways,
In the quietude of awareness, we stay.

A Symphony of Inner Truths

Within the heart, a melody plays,
A symphony of truths and rays.
With every note, the spirit sings,
Unlocking all that freedom brings.

In quiet moments, wisdom calls,
Echoing softly through the halls.
Each truth unveiled, a guiding light,
In harmony, we find our sight.

The rhythm flows, both loud and meek,
In every silence, echoes speak.
A dance of feelings, sharp and pure,
In the symphony, we find our cure.

Together we weave our tales so bright,
In every chord, a spark of light.
As passions rise, the heart knows best,
In the symphony of truths, we rest.

With open minds and hearts laid bare,
We share the music found in care.
Within us lies a sacred truth,
A symphony of inner truths.

Crystalline Insights

Glimmers dance on frosted glass,
Truths unfold, they slowly pass.
Shadows flicker, whispers chime,
In this crystal, thoughts sublime.

Fragments shine in radiant light,
Secrets hidden, out of sight.
Each reflection, a story told,
With every shard, a dream unfolds.

Colors bleed in twilight's grasp,
Moments caught within the clasp.
Nature's mirror, pure and clear,
Reflecting all that we hold dear.

Wisdom blooms in fractured space,
Beauty found in every trace.
Cascades of thoughts, like water flow,
In crystalline depths, insights grow.

Embrace the shards that glimmer bright,
Illuminate the endless night.
With every piece, a part of time,
In crystalline form, we rise and climb.

Threads of Fate

Woven strands in twilight's loom,
Destinies whisper, dispel the gloom.
In tangled paths, we find our place,
Each twist and turn, a fated trace.

Colors merge to form our tale,
Silent pacts that never pale.
Hearts connect and journeys blend,
In this tapestry, we transcend.

Fingers brush across the seams,
Weaving hopes, stitching dreams.
With every thread, a life connects,
A dance of fate, new paths direct.

Unraveled fears, entwined with grace,
In every knot, a saving embrace.
As the fabric sways and bends,
Threads of fate, where journey ends.

Together we craft a vivid weave,
In silent strength, we believe.
Embrace the threads that pull us near,
Life's rich fabric, ever dear.

Gentle Reminders of Being

In moments soft, we pause and breathe,
The world whispers truths we often leave.
Amidst the noise, a quiet song,
Reminds us where our hearts belong.

Like petals falling from a tree,
Life's beauty blooms in simplicity.
Each step a dance, each breath a gift,
A gentle wave, a soothing lift.

In silence found, we hear the call,
Of nature's pulse that binds us all.
With every dawn, new hope will rise,
An endless sky, a canvas wide.

Embrace the now, let go of pain,
In every loss, something to gain.
For in the stillness, love will weave,
A tapestry of dreams we believe.

So take a moment, close your eyes,
And seek the spark within the skies.
For life is fleeting, a gentle breeze,
Each heartbeat echoes with sweet reprise.

Clarity Beyond the Veil

Through fog and haze, the vision clears,
Awakens dreams that draw us near.
The path unknown, yet brightly lit,
With every step, our spirits fit.

In shadows cast, we find the light,
A flame within that ignites the night.
Our fears dissolve, like mist in sun,
A journey shared, two become one.

Beyond the veil, the truth awaits,
With open hearts, we navigate fates.
Each breath a beacon, shining bright,
Guides us through the darkest night.

With every moment, lessons gleam,
Transforming life into a dream.
Let intuition lead the way,
In stillness found, we softly sway.

For clarity blooms in gentle ways,
Through trials faced, a soul's embrace.
Embrace the journey, trust the rise,
For in the light, the spirit flies.

Flickering Lanterns in the Dark

In the stillness of the night,
Lanterns flicker soft and bright.
Each glow a whisper, guiding true,
Through shadows deep, to paths anew.

Winds may howl, and storms may rage,
Yet hope can light a brand new page.
For every tear, a spark ignites,
A dance of dreams, in starry nights.

With every flicker, stories live,
Of love and loss, the strength to give.
In darkness deep, we find our way,
Illuminated hearts shall stay.

Together we stand under the sky,
With lanterns raised, we soar and fly.
Bound by the warmth of human grace,
In light's embrace, we find our place.

So as we walk this winding lane,
Let flickering hopes extinguish pain.
For in the dark, we'll bravely spark,
A brighter dawn, a path to embark.

The Silent Compass

In quiet moments, we can find,
A compass hidden in the mind.
With every pulse, it points the way,
Guiding hearts through night and day.

Each choice a step, each thought a guide,
In stillness, wisdom won't confide.
For when we listen, truth unfolds,
The compass shows what love beholds.

Through storms we sail, through calm we glide,
With faith as anchor, we abide.
Where doubts may dwell, hope shines so clear,
The compass whispers, drawing near.

In pathways crossed, we find our seat,
Of destiny, the chance to meet.
For every turn, a chance to grow,
In silence deep, the heart will know.

So trust the voice that calls you home,
The silent compass, lest you roam.
In gentle nudges, life directs,
In every choice, the soul connects.

Underneath the Cascades

Water rushes down the stone,
Whispers of the wild unknown,
Nature's lullaby in tune,
Beneath the sun, beneath the moon.

Footfalls soft on mossy ground,
In this haven, peace is found,
Leaves above in swaying dance,
Life unfolds in every glance.

Echoes of a distant call,
Cascades hear the stories fall,
Hidden paths, a journey's quest,
Every step—a soul's unrest.

Sunlight dapples through the trees,
Carried gently by the breeze,
Moments linger, time stands still,
Underneath the mountain's will.

In this realm where spirits roam,
Nature's heart feels like our home,
Beneath the cascades, we belong,
Wrapped in nature's timeless song.

Depths of the Unsaid

Silence holds a heavy weight,
Words unspoken, sealed by fate,
Eyes that speak in quiet tones,
Hidden truths, yet to be known.

Longing glances cross the space,
In the depths, we seek the grace,
Heartbeats echo what we feel,
In this hush, the pain is real.

Moments sigh, they linger here,
In the shadows, love and fear,
Like a secret held too tight,
In the depths of darkest night.

Hope emerges through the gloom,
In the void, there blooms a room,
For the words we dare not say,
In the silence, they will stay.

Depths of feelings, vast and wide,
In the quiet, truths abide,
Together we can find the way,
Through the depths, come what may.

The Secret Chord

In the shadows of the night,
Music whispers, pure delight,
Strumming soft on heartstrings tight,
In the silence, sparks ignite.

Each note carries dreams untold,
Melodies in curves unfold,
In the hush, the spirit sways,
Finding peace in hidden ways.

Through the gaps of time we glean,
Echoes of what might have been,
Every chord a breath, a sigh,
In the music, we can fly.

The air vibrates with the sound,
In each heartbeat, we are bound,
Notes entwined, they draw us near,
In the rhythm, love appears.

When the world feels steeped in gray,
Find the secret chord today,
Let it guide you through the strife,
In that sound, discover life.

Touches of Rawness

Rugged edges, truth laid bare,
In the chaos, feelings share,
Unpolished, yet so real,
In the raw, the heart can heal.

Moments stripped of all disguise,
Vulnerability, so wise,
Every flaw a tale to tell,
In the deep, we rise and fell.

Textures rough against the skin,
Life exposed, where we begin,
In the tangled mess of now,
Find the strength to take a bow.

Through the cracks, the light pours in,
In the brave, we shed our sin,
Do not fear the scars you wear,
In the rawness, love lays bare.

Touches fleeting, moments cling,
In the heart, we find our spring,
Embrace the chaos, unrefined,
In the rawness, truth we find.

Fragments of the Unseen

In shadows dance the silent dreams,
Whispers lost in moonlit streams.
Fleeting glimpses, echoes wane,
Piecing fragments, hope in vain.

A tapestry of thoughts, we weave,
Beneath the surface, we believe.
Each secret hid, a tale untold,
In the heart, the warmth of gold.

Time pauses, then it flies,
Beneath the stars, the truth belies.
Faces blend in twilight's glow,
Mysteries in what we know.

With every breath, we chase the night,
In stillness, find the hidden light.
Through aching voids of dark and fear,
Unseen worlds, they linger near.

Embrace the silence, let it sing,
In the quiet, hope takes wing.
Fragments gather, dreams align,
In unseen worlds, we find the sign.

A Symphony of Truths

Melodies weave in twilight's haze,
Notes collide in the evening's gaze.
Harmonies blend with whispered sighs,
In the heart, the music flies.

Each truth a note, a tale to tell,
Rising rhythms, a sacred swell.
In every chord, a life unfolds,
In the silence, the heart holds.

The dance of shadows, light, and sound,
In every echo, hope is found.
Together we move, a solemn grace,
In the symphony, we find our place.

The winds carry the songs of old,
Tales of warmth in the bitter cold.
Resonating through the night,
A tapestry of purest light.

Let the symphony wash our fears,
In each note, a thousand years.
With open hearts, we'll play our part,
In the music, we find the heart.

Navigating the Unheard

In silence, paths begin to form,
Waves of thought, gentle yet warm.
Navigating through the unseen,
In quiet moments, we glean.

Voices whisper in the night,
Guiding souls toward the light.
Lost in echoes, shadows sway,
Finding strength in what's today.

With every heartbeat, step anew,
In stillness, hopes come into view.
The unseen guides the way we tread,
In every breath, the dreams we've bred.

Every moment, a thought to chase,
Navigating through time and space.
In the journey, we seek to find,
The unheard truth, both brave and kind.

Let the whispers lead us home,
In the unspoken, hearts will roam.
Through the quiet, we will see,
The beauty in what's meant to be.

Eclipsed Radiance

A shadow falls, the light retreats,
In dusks embrace, our heartbeat meets.
Whispers of the past collide,
In eclipsed radiance, we confide.

Hope flickers like a distant star,
Guiding us through night's bizarre.
In every dark, the spark is found,
In silence, we hear the sound.

Waves of shadows lap the shore,
In twilight's grasp, we search for more.
Each glimmer holds a tale of loss,
In the eclipse, we bear the cross.

Yet from the dark, the dawn will rise,
Illuminating painted skies.
In the stillness, our spirits soar,
Eclipsed radiance, forevermore.

With every eclipse, we learn to see,
The beauty in what's meant to be.
In shadows deep, our faith ignites,
Eclipsed radiance in starry nights.

Tides of Understanding

Waves that whisper secrets true,
Gentle caresses on the shore,
Understanding comes in hues,
As tides retreat, they ask for more.

Pebbles scattered, stories told,
In each moment, lessons grow,
Softly, time begins to mold,
A deeper bond we come to know.

In moonlight's glow, we find our place,
Reflections dance upon the sea,
A journey joined, a sacred space,
Where tides align with you and me.

Echoes of the heart resound,
Each wave, a chance to start anew,
In understanding's arms, we're found,
The ocean sings, we feel it too.

As daylight fades, the stars awake,
A silent pact we seal tonight,
With each ebbing, there's a stake,
In tides of understanding, we unite.

The Subtle Art of Knowing

In whispers soft, we find the light,
Truth unfolds in gentle ways,
The subtle art, a quiet sight,
Awakens dreams of brighter days.

Between the lines, we seek to see,
The nuances that life can bring,
Each moment's gift is meant to be,
A melody in silence sings.

With every glance, a story shared,
Our hearts entwined in rich discourse,
The art of knowing, deeply paired,
In trust we find the hidden source.

Fleeting shadows, thoughts converge,
A dance of minds, a sweet pursuit,
In stillness, we begin to surge,
To understand the heart's salute.

As twilight falls, the canvas spreads,
Colors blend, the world awakes,
In knowing's grasp, our path treads,
The subtle art in life's heartaches.

Voices in the Stillness

In the stillness, whispers rise,
Voices echo through the night,
Secrets shared beneath the skies,
In silence, we find pure light.

Each heartbeat tells a tale untold,
A canvas painted with our truth,
In quiet moments, brave and bold,
We touch the essence of our youth.

Listen close, for wisdom's call,
In the hush, we find our way,
Through shadows deep, we stand tall,
Voices guide us, come what may.

The softest sounds bring forth our dreams,
A symphony of souls combined,
In stillness lived, the heart redeems,
The voices of the purest kind.

As dawn approaches, silence fades,
Yet still the echoes linger near,
In every heartbeat, truth cascades,
Voices whisper, forever clear.

Clarity's Gentle Call

In morning mist, a soft embrace,
Clarity whispers close to me,
A gentle nudge in time and space,
I find my thoughts begin to see.

Through tangled paths, the fog will part,
Each step revealing what was lost,
With open mind, I guard my heart,
In clarity, we weigh the cost.

The sun alights on wisdom's shore,
A beacon bright, it lights the way,
Inviting me to seek for more,
In every moment, come what may.

With every breath, the vision grows,
A world awakened to my soul,
Through clarity, my spirit flows,
I discover what makes me whole.

And as the day begins to wane,
Clarity's call, my guiding star,
In every thought, there's joy and pain,
To follow truth, no matter how far.

Threads of Hidden Knowledge

In whispered tones the secrets weave,
A tapestry of truths we conceive.
Each thread a story, bold yet shy,
Entwined in silence, they softly lie.

The ancients spoke in riddles profound,
Their wisdom lost, yet still can be found.
Beneath the layers, the whispers grow,
In the heart of the seeker, they brightly glow.

From shadows deep, the echoes call,
A dance of light, a rise, a fall.
With every stitch, enlightenment's wait,
Threads of knowledge, shared by fate.

Through the ages, the lessons unfold,
In every moment, the brave and bold.
The fabric of time, a guide for the wise,
Threads of hidden knowledge, beneath our skies.

Breathe in the tales of those gone by,
Listen closely, let your spirit fly.
For every thread, a gift to behold,
The wisdom of ages, worth far more than gold.

Silent Testimonies

In every corner, shadows lie still,
Witness to moments, against their will.
A sigh of sorrow, a whispering plea,
Silent testimonies, yearning to be free.

The walls have ears, they've heard it all,
Stories of triumphs, and how we fall.
Echoes of laughter carried on wind,
The silent witnesses, our lives rescind.

They hold our dreams and our deepest fears,
A library of hearts, soaked in our tears.
Yet in their silence, a truth remains,
Testimonies written in joy and pains.

When night descends, the world takes a rest,
These silent tales are at their best.
In the twilight glow, memories arise,
Silent testimonies dance in our eyes.

Listen closely, for the stories they tell,
A chronicle rich, where silence dwells.
For every heartbeat, every sigh,
Silent testimonies never truly die.

The Language of Shadows

In twilight's embrace, shadows take form,
They speak in silence, a soft, gentle warmth.
With gestures and glances, a story is spun,
The language of shadows, where all is begun.

Through flickering light, the dark whispers flow,
Telling of secrets that we may not know.
A dance of the unseen, profound yet shy,
In silent dialogues, night learns to fly.

Every corner they touch, a tale is unfurled,
In the quiet depths, a concealed world.
With every flicker, a mystery unfolds,
The language of shadows, a wonder of old.

From dusk until dawn, they weave and entwine,
In the heart of the night, their stories align.
A world uncharted, where the brave dare glance,
The language of shadows invites us to dance.

So heed the whispers, don't turn away,
For in the darkness, shadows play.
A symphony written in shades and hues,
The language of shadows—the muse we choose.

Beneath the Surface

In calm waters where secrets dwell,
Lies a world of stories, hard to tell.
Beneath the surface, shadows dance,
A hidden realm where dreams advance.

Each ripple whispers of tales untold,
Of hopes and fears, both timid and bold.
The peace of silence hides a storm,
Beneath the surface, where currents warm.

A treasure trove of hearts concealed,
In hushed tones, the truth is revealed.
Dive deeper still, embrace the unknown,
Beneath the surface, seeds of love are sown.

In the quiet depths, reflections glow,
The depths of our souls, a place to grow.
Surface calm belies the waves' embrace,
Beneath the surface, we find our place.

Explore the waters, venture inside,
For beneath the surface, magic does hide.
There lies a journey, vast and wide,
Beneath the surface, let dreams collide.

Whispers of the Earth

In the morning light, a gentle sigh,
Nature speaks softly, as time drifts by.
Leaves dance lightly on the breeze,
A symphony calls, a heart at ease.

Mountains stand tall, guardians of past,
Each echo a story, shadows are cast.
Rivers weave tales through valleys wide,
Whispers of wisdom in currents glide.

The soil breathes life, rich and deep,
Nurturing dreams that quietly sleep.
Under the surface, secrets lay,
In every heartbeat, they find their way.

Dewdrops shimmer at dawn's first light,
Glistening jewels that end the night.
Nature's poetry can softly heal,
In every moment, our souls reveal.

Shadows of Pure Essence

Beneath the moon's glow, whispers conspire,
Shadows dance lightly, stoking the fire.
In the stillness, secrets take flight,
Veils of the night, cloaked in delight.

Echoes of laughter, a fleeting trace,
In shadows we find a familiar face.
Each flicker of light tells a tale,
Of dreams that linger—soft winds prevail.

Fragments of memory, lost in the fold,
Shadows reveal what the heart has told.
In silence we wander, searching for grace,
In the depths of darkness, we find our place.

A dance of reflections, timeless and clear,
In each fleeting moment, essence draws near.
The beauty in shadows, a gift to behold,
A tapestry woven, with threads of gold.

The Calm Before the Reveal

A stillness lingers, thick in the air,
Breath held tight, a moment rare.
The world pauses, in anxious wait,
As destiny whispers, tempting fate.

Clouds gather soft, like dreams unspun,
A canvas of silence before the run.
In the heartbeats, tension unfolds,
The promise of change in secrets told.

A gentle rustle in the waiting trees,
Preludes to chaos, soft as a breeze.
The hush holds power, grows ever strong,
In the calmness, we learn where we belong.

With every heartbeat, a story unfurls,
A truth that dances, in rippling swirls.
In the pause, we breathe in the chance,
To embrace the unknown, to boldly dance.

Conversations with the Invisible

In the silence, a voice can be found,
Whispers of hearts, where thoughts abound.
Between the moments, we seek and yearn,
For the hidden truth that we discern.

The air vibrates with unspoken dreams,
Echoes of laughter, or so it seems.
Messages linger just out of sight,
Meeting our souls in the soft moonlight.

In shadows we mingle, in dreams we play,
Conversations weave through night and day.
The invisible speaks in shimmering thread,
Unraveling stories that dance in our head.

A flicker, a spark, a thought shared anew,
In the spaces between, our spirits flew.
With every heartbeat, our souls engage,
In dialogues deep, we turn the page.

Half-Truths and Shadows

In the twilight's fading grace,
Secrets linger in the space,
Whispers dance on silent streams,
Half-truths weave in fractured dreams.

Shadows play on truth's facade,
Echoes murmur, soft and odd,
Beliefs cast long, deceptive light,
Hiding fears of endless night.

Masks adorned in painted smiles,
Hide the pain that stretches miles,
Yet beneath the veils we wear,
Truth resides, a silent prayer.

Fragments lost in endless chase,
Blur the lines of time and space,
Each step taken, filled with doubt,
Seeking what we're all about.

In the stillness, shadows part,
Revealing echoes of the heart,
Half-truths fade in morning's glow,
Leaving wisdom in their flow.

Unspoken Bonds of Light

In the quiet of our ties,
Words unspoken fill the skies,
Hearts entwined in silent grace,
A dance of love we can't erase.

Fingers brush in gentle touch,
Unseen bonds that mean so much,
Every glance a shared delight,
In the shadows, purest light.

Distance fades where spirits soar,
Trusting sails on unseen shore,
In the hush, our stories blend,
Whispers soft, the perfect mend.

Light connects what words can't say,
Guiding us along the way,
In the silence, hearts ignite,
Building dreams on wings of light.

Through the dark, we find our way,
Bonds unspoken, bright as day,
In the depths, the brightest shine,
Love and truth forever intertwine.

Tides of Sincerity

Waves roll in with gentle grace,
Carrying truth to every place,
Tides of honesty arise,
Cleansing hearts beneath the skies.

In the depths where secrets sleep,
Sincerity runs strong and deep,
Churning forth with every rise,
Washing shores of painted lies.

The moon, a guide in endless night,
Illuminates what feels so right,
In each ebb, a promise found,
As tides dance to a soulful sound.

Drifting thoughts like boats afloat,
Carry dreams on words we wrote,
Every swell, a testament,
To the depths of our content.

As oceans meet the skies above,
Waves reflect the strength of love,
In tides of truth, we find our way,
Embracing dawn of each new day.

Resonant Echoes in the Stillness

In the stillness where we pause,
Echoes linger, hushed applause,
Moments shared in silent breath,
Resonate beyond our death.

Each heartbeat a distant sound,
Whispers linger, profound,
In the quiet, voices blend,
Carving space where dreams transcend.

Still waters hide profound thoughts,
In their depth, the wisdom sought,
Ripples form where silence grows,
Sowing seeds of calm repose.

Time dissolves in gentle waves,
Sounding tones of quiet graves,
In the echoes, stories thrive,
Whispers of what keeps us alive.

Resonance in every sigh,
Bonds that reach beyond the sky,
In stillness, love finds its place,
In echoes, we leave our trace.

A Canvas of Nuance

Brushstrokes blend in soft embrace,
Colors dance in timeless grace.
Whispers echo through the hue,
A story lives in shades anew.

Each layer tells a silent tale,
Of sunlit hills and twilight pale.
In silence, frames of dreams collide,
A canvas where the heart can abide.

Textures weave a rich delight,
In every corner, shadows light.
From chaos blooms a perfect form,
A stillness held in gentle storm.

The artist's hand in quiet pause,
Crafts a world without a cause.
In strokes of thought, the mind takes flight,
A canvas glows with inner light.

Here beauty lies, both raw and true,
In depths of paint, a vision grew.
Through each exploration, love expands,
A canvas born from tender hands.

Faint Trails of Authenticity

Footprints linger on the ground,
In whispers soft, their stories found.
Meandering paths through time's embrace,
Faint trails mark a hidden grace.

In quietude, the heart aligns,
With echoes of the past entwined.
Each line a truth, each step a sigh,
Authenticity will never die.

In shadows cast by fleeting light,
The journey shapes what feels so right.
Through tangled woods, the spirit roams,
In every turn, it finds its home.

Fragrant blooms and whispered dreams,
Reveal the layers, like sunlit beams.
The art of being, unmasked, unchained,
In faint trails, the soul unfeigned.

Let the world see what once was lost,
In humble paths, no matter the cost.
Authentic steps upon this earth,
Reclaiming every last true worth.

The Quiet Path

Amidst the trees, a whisper clear,
The quiet path draws ever near.
Soft moss cradles weary feet,
In solitude, the heartbeat's beat.

Sunlight filters through the leaves,
In tranquil breaths, the spirit weaves.
Nature's hymn, a soothing song,
On this path, we all belong.

Cool breezes carry thoughts away,
Each step a dance, a chance to sway.
In silence, wisdom takes its place,
A gentle touch, a warm embrace.

Through winding trails, the heart can roam,
Finding peace, the soul's true home.
With every turn, a breath of grace,
The quiet path, a sacred space.

Moments pause, as shadows play,
In nature's hands, we find our way.
With every footfall, hope ignites,
On this road, our spirit lights.

Harbingers of Reality

In whispers soft, the truth unfolds,
Harbingers come, with tales untold.
They walk the line, both near and far,
Shining bright like guiding stars.

Through mirrored glass, reflections gleam,
Waking life from hidden dream.
In echoes loud and shadows cast,
The essence of the now holds fast.

With every breath, they call our name,
Unraveling doubts, igniting flame.
Each moment's choice a thread in time,
With every heartbeat, life can rhyme.

The veil is lifted, eyes awake,
To see the paths we long to take.
In visions clear, we find our way,
Harbingers lead us into day.

Reality shifts in subtle grace,
As we welcome change to embrace.
With open hearts, the journey's begun,
In truth and light, we are all one.

Subtle Hints of Reality

In shadows cast, the truth lies low,
A whisper soft that we must know.
It dances lightly in the air,
An echo faint, a silent prayer.

Through fleeting dreams, we chase the light,
In every corner, day and night.
A fleeting glance, a knowing gaze,
We find our path in winding ways.

The heart perceives what eyes can't see,
In nature's song, we find our plea.
A subtle hint, a chance to grow,
With every step, we learn to flow.

In moments still, the world reveals,
The layers deep, the truth it seals.
A gentle push, a soft caress,
In quietude, we find our quest.

So take a breath, and heed the call,
For life is but a fleeting ball.
Embrace the hints, the signs unfold,
In subtlety, our dreams are told.

Threads of Insight

From deepest thoughts, ideas arise,
A tapestry spun beneath blue skies.
Each thread unique, a story shared,
In woven paths, our fates declared.

Like rivers flow through ancient lands,
The wisdom ripe in steady hands.
Each twist and turn reveals a truth,
A dance of ages, eternal youth.

In every stitch, a spark ignites,
A flash of knowledge, guiding lights.
With open hearts, we dare to see,
The intricate weave of life's decree.

Through gentle whispers, insights gleam,
In moments soft, we find our dream.
Embrace each thread, let go of fear,
For through connection, love draws near.

So gather close, let's pull the strands,
Together, weaving with our hands.
With all our strength, the fabric grows,
In unity, our vision flows.

The Unseen Tapestry

In hidden realms, the threads entwine,
Crafting stories, divine design.
An unseen force from years gone by,
Guides our steps as time slips by.

Each moment captured, a stitch in time,
The highs, the lows, the pure sublime.
With every heartbeat, patterns form,
A dance of chaos, a gentle storm.

As colors merge, the picture grows,
In every shadow, the radiance glows.
Life's rich tapestry unveils its art,
In quiet corners of the heart.

So take a glance at what lies beneath,
The hidden links, the tales they sheath.
Within the strands, the answers bloom,
In woven shadows, we discard gloom.

Embrace the unseen, let your heart soar,
In unity, we unlock the door.
Together we weave, in love's sweet play,
A tapestry rich, come what may.

Shimmers of Integrity

In every glance, a truth reflected,
A steadfast heart, the soul detected.
Through trials faced and battles fought,
The light of honor, never bought.

With gentle steps, we pave the road,
As values shine, our heavy load.
Integrity, a guiding star,
Illuminates the journey far.

In choice and voice, our strength we find,
A beacon bright, forever kind.
When shadows loom and doubts arise,
We stand as one, 'neath open skies.

With every breath, we breathe our truth,
In love's embrace lies lasting proof.
Through challenges, we rise and stand,
In shimmers bold, we make our brand.

So let us walk with courage high,
Through storms and sun, we will not die.
For in the heart of those who care,
Integrity shimmers everywhere.

The Softest Light of Understanding

In shadows cast by doubt's embrace,
A candle flickers, finds its place.
With every whisper, fears unwind,
The softest light, it gently binds.

In moments shared, we start to see,
The depths of hearts, the yearnings free.
A glance exchanged, a nod of grace,
Brings warmth within this sacred space.

Through stories told, we weave a thread,
A tapestry of words unsaid.
In silence sweet, connection grows,
With tender truths, our wisdom flows.

As understanding softly blooms,
It scatters light in darker rooms.
Each spark ignites a soothing flame,
And lights the path to love's sweet name.

Amidst the noise, a stillness found,
In gentle words, our souls are crowned.
For in this light, we find our way,
To brighter dawns and warmer days.

Revealed in Solitude

Within the stillness, shadows play,
In quiet corners where thoughts stray.
A mirror shows what lies inside,
In solitude, our truths abide.

Each moment spent, a treasure gained,
In silent halls, where hearts are trained.
A whisper speaks of dreams anew,
Revealing what we never knew.

The world outside can fade away,
As inward journeys start to sway.
With every breath, the past unfolds,
In solitude, our spirit holds.

The echoes of the heart resound,
In sacred spaces, peace is found.
Where solitude becomes our guide,
The depths of self we cannot hide.

In gentle hours, we come alive,
As within, our hopes derive.
Connection blooms when we're alone,
In solitude, we're never thrown.

Echoes Beneath the Silence

In quiet moments, whispers loom,
Within the hush, deep thoughts consume.
A heartbeat thuds like distant drums,
With echoes soft, the silence hums.

Between the lines of what we say,
The truths emerge in subtle sway.
Each pause a chance for meaning sparked,
In silence, worlds are deeply marked.

The shadows blend with evening light,
As echoes roam, both day and night.
A lingering thought, a smile's trace,
Beneath the silence, we find grace.

In every sigh, the past remains,
Each memory, like gentle rains.
Through silence, bonds are redefined,
In echoes deep, our hearts aligned.

So let us dwell in quiet space,
Where echoes show a soft embrace.
For in the silent, we are free,
To hear the heart's own symphony.

The Gentle Pull of Genuineness

Amidst the noise, a tender call,
The gentle pull that stirs us all.
In every glance, a truth revealed,
With open hearts, our wounds are healed.

A smile exchanged, the world ignites,
With genuine warmth, we shine our lights.
In honest words, connections form,
The gentle pull, a soothing storm.

In giving space, we find our ground,
In every moment, love is found.
With authenticity as our guide,
The gentle pull will not divide.

In laughter shared and sorrows shared,
The spirit's spark is truly bared.
Each story told, a thread we mend,
In genuineness, we find a friend.

So let us dance in truth's embrace,
With loyalty and boundless grace.
For in the pull of hearts sincere,
We find our place, our vision clear.

Beneath the Surface

In the depths, shadows play,
Whispers dance, drift away.
Secrets lie in muted tones,
Beneath the stone, the heart moans.

Waves break, a muted roar,
The unseen calls for more.
Fingers trace the cold, dark sea,
Yearning for what cannot be.

Tides shift in a silent play,
Dreams swim, yet go astray.
Invisible threads hold tight,
Guiding souls through the night.

Ebb and flow, silence weaves,
Hidden tales that each heart cleaves.
From the dark, truth will emerge,
Breaking free, a gentle surge.

Crystals form on the sea floor,
Echoes calling evermore.
In the silence, life finds grace,
Beneath the surface, we embrace.

The Unvoiced Confessions

In the quiet of the night,
Fears linger, out of sight.
Words unspoken, heavy heart,
Yearning for a brand new start.

Eyes meet, a silent plea,
Voices lost, yet still free.
Tangled truths, shadows blend,
In the silence, we pretend.

Pages turned with ink of pain,
Stories etched, yet remain.
In the depth, a longing sigh,
To be heard, to touch the sky.

Hearts whisper in the dark,
Echoes left a tender mark.
Unvoiced dreams hang in the air,
Hope resides within despair.

Each heartbeat a confession,
Laden with suppressed expression.
In the stillness, light can creep,
Awakening the vows we keep.

Flickers of Clarity

In the haze, a shadow blooms,
Flickering light dispels the glooms.
Thoughts drift like leaves on streams,
Catching whispers, saving dreams.

A candle flickers, soft and bright,
Piercing through the thickest night.
Moments shrink, yet expand,
Grasping truths, a steady hand.

Through the fog, horizons clear,
Fears dissolve as hope draws near.
In the quiet, wisdom speaks,
Guiding hearts, though time feels weak.

Flickers dance in the mind's eye,
Illuminating reasons why.
With each spark, a path unfolds,
Stories waiting to be told.

Chasing shadows, we will find,
In the dark, a light unconfined.
Flickers bright, like starlight's sway,
Turning night into day.

Silent Declarations

In the void, intentions soar,
Words unspoken, promise more.
Glimmers of what lies within,
Silent vows where love begins.

In the stillness, moments freeze,
Feelings rise upon the breeze.
Hands held tight, hearts beat loud,
Courage wrapped in a shroud.

Truth lingers in the air we breathe,
Untold tales that hearts believe.
In each glance, worlds collide,
Echoes of love, deep inside.

A soft touch, a knowing glance,
Silent declarations, a dance.
In the hush, where shadows blend,
Promises made that won't rescind.

With every heartbeat, a refrain,
Binding souls in joy and pain.
In the silence, love's embrace,
Silent truths we dare to face.

Soft Echoes on a Winter's Night

Snowflakes dance in moonlit air,
Whispers soft, a gentle prayer.
Through the pines, the shadows play,
Night unfolds in silver gray.

Frosted breath hangs in the breeze,
Nature's hush, the heart it frees.
Footsteps crunch on frozen ground,
In this peace, true solace found.

Stars above in velvet skies,
Dreams take flight, the spirit flies.
Each echo sings a tale of old,
In this moment, warmth unfolds.

Crimson fires in cabins glow,
Fingers curled, their warmth they show.
Laughter weaves through cozy nights,
Soft echoes, the heart ignites.

As dawn breaks, the colors blend,
A canvas formed where snowflakes end.
The winter's night, a memory bright,
Soft echoes linger, pure delight.

Reflective Shades of Truth

In quiet depths, we seek the real,
Beneath the surface, layers peel.
Truth resides in shadows cast,
In whispers soft, not loud nor fast.

Mirrors show what we suppress,
Each crack reveals the heart's distress.
Yet in the light, new faces dawn,
Reflections form as dusk moves on.

Colors fade, yet truths remain,
Emotions throb, a gentle pain.
Searching eyes, they long to see,
The vivid shades of what can be.

Through tangled paths of hope and fear,
We chase the voices, drawing near.
In every twist, a lesson learned,
With every step, the heart has turned.

Embrace the light, accept the night,
In shades of truth, we find our sight.
The complexity, a woven thread,
In reflective depths, we are led.

Unraveled Threads

Threads of time, so finely spun,
Each moment lost, a race we run.
Frayed and tangled, life's design,
An intricate web, both yours and mine.

Memories woven, colors fade,
In shadows long where dreams are laid.
Each stitch a tale, of love and loss,
Unraveled now, we bear the cross.

In silence, echoes softly call,
To join the dance, to rise, to fall.
A tapestry of joys and fears,
Stitched with laughter, soaked in tears.

Weaving back the frayed ends tight,
Searching for meaning in the night.
In every thread, a life embraced,
The stories left can't be replaced.

Embrace the art of what's undone,
In all the flaws, new threads begun.
The beauty lies in what we see,
Unraveled threads, we set them free.

Ethereal Calls of Reality

In breathless dreams, we float away,
To realms where shadows gently play.
Ethereal whispers weave through strands,
Calling forth the heart's demands.

Graceful forms in twilight haze,
Guide us through the misty maze.
In echoes soft, the truths unfold,
A story written, yet untold.

Threads of light and dark entwine,
In every moment, fate aligns.
Reality dances in a breeze,
In stillness found beneath the trees.

Awakened souls, we seek the light,
In all the chaos, find our sight.
Calls of nature, pure and free,
In every heartbeat, we agree.

To live within the sacred now,
To breathe, to learn, to humbly bow.
Ethereal dances mark the way,
Toward the dawn of each new day.

Echoes of Honesty

In the stillness, words unfold,
Truths untold, softly bold.
Reflections dance in silent air,
Whispers linger, hearts laid bare.

Promises hang like fragile threads,
Bonds of trust, where silence treads.
In every glance, a story glows,
A canvas rich, where honesty shows.

Voices mingle in twilight's hue,
Gentle sighs, a fleeting view.
Echoes chase through time's embrace,
Finding solace in truth's grace.

Hands held tight against the night,
Guided by the inner light.
Even shadows cannot conceal,
What the heart longs to reveal.

In the dusk, where secrets fade,
The warmth of trust is gently laid.
Echoes whisper, soft and clear,
In the silence, love draws near.

Secrets in the Shadows

Beneath the moon's soft silver glow,
Lies a realm where few can go.
Whispers blend with the night's embrace,
Secrets hidden, a sacred space.

Fingers trace the edges blurred,
In hushed tones, soft voices stirred.
Among the trees, time stands still,
Unveiling dreams, unveiling will.

Glimmers dance upon the ground,
In darkness, whispers all around.
Every tale a thread of fate,
In shadows deep, we contemplate.

Silhouettes move under starry skies,
Secrets linger, where silence lies.
In the hush, a heartbeat speaks,
Finding truth in what it seeks.

Through hidden paths, we dare to tread,
Following trails of unspoken dread.
Yet in the dark, a light prevails,
Guiding us through night's soft veils.

Veils of Revelation

Amidst the fog, a dawn appears,
Lifting veils of buried fears.
New colors burst, horizons wide,
Revelations no longer hide.

Each moment sings a muted song,
Harmony where we belong.
With every step, the truth unspools,
In the light, we find the jewels.

Shadows shift and merge as one,
Echoes dance in the rising sun.
Layers peel, the heart exposed,
In vulnerability, we are rose.

Through trials faced, we bear our scars,
Stories etched like ancient stars.
Every tear, a glimpse of grace,
In revealing, we find our place.

Veils lift high, revealing all,
In the quiet, answers call.
In the truth, we find connection,
In revelation, deep reflection.

Murmurs of the Heart

In every heartbeat, secrets flow,
A silent tune, a soft hello.
Murmurs echo through the night,
Carrying dreams toward the light.

Emotions rise like ocean tides,
Waves of hope that gently slide.
In every sigh, a story's spun,
In whispered breaths, we become one.

A gentle clash of minds and souls,
Filling spaces, making whole.
With every glance, a tale ignites,
Painting love in vibrant lights.

Through shadows cast and laughter shared,
In the dance, we are declared.
Murmurs guide us, soft and clear,
In the depths, we hold what's dear.

Trust the whispers of the night,
Feel the warmth, embrace the light.
For in those murmurs, truth will start,
A bond unbroken, the world's heart.

The Melody of Unveilings

In shadows deep where secrets lie,
The whispers call, the echoes sigh.
Each note a tale, each chord a dream,
Unseen worlds brought forth to gleam.

With gentle hands, the silence breaks,
A melody of hope awakes.
The heart responds, a tender throng,
In every note, we find our song.

Through veils of mist, the voices rise,
Like fleeting glimpses of the skies.
Harmonies of truth, they weave,
A tapestry we dare believe.

In moments soft, the air is filled,
With every sigh, our souls are thrilled.
A symphony of light and shade,
Unveiling dreams that never fade.

So let the music take its course,
With every pulse, a vital force.
In stillness found, our spirits soar,
In melody, we are much more.

Notes of Subtlety

In hushed tones of the evening air,
Whispers linger, secrets rare.
A gentle breeze, a fleeting thought,
Subtle hints in silence caught.

Each glance exchanged, a silent plea,
In between, what's yet to see.
Delicate threads that tightly bind,
The unspoken, intertwined.

Beneath the surface, ripples play,
In quiet corners, shadows sway.
Hints of laughter, traces here,
A canvas stretched, emotions clear.

With every pause, a chance to feel,
A delicate dance, the subtle reel.
Layers peeled with gentle grace,
Inviting all to embrace the space.

So listen close, to heartbeats near,
In quietude, the truths appear.
In every note, a world resides,
A symphony where magic hides.

Between the Words

In silence held, a story breathes,
Beyond the lines, the heart believes.
Each pause a canvas, brushed with care,
Between the words, we find our share.

The spaces speak, where thoughts reside,
A world unsung, yet pulsing wide.
With every sigh, a tale unfolds,
In whispers soft, the truth beholds.

A glance can say what words can't find,
In fleeting moments, love is blind.
A look, a gesture, softly shared,
In silent realms, our souls repaired.

With every phrase, the echoes swell,
In hidden depths, our dreams compel.
Beyond the syntax, feelings flow,
In every silence, there's much to know.

So gather close, and hear the space,
Where meaning dwells, and hearts embrace.
In every heartbeat, a pulse of truth,
Between the words, we find our youth.

A Dance of Hidden Depths

In shadows cast by the waning light,
A dance begins, both soft and bright.
With every step, a secret sway,
In hidden depths, we drift away.

The rhythm flows like a gentle tide,
In every turn, where dreams abide.
With graceful spins, we intertwine,
In whispered grace, the stars align.

Each heartbeat echoes, a silent drum,
Inviting all to join the fun.
In hidden layers, stories blend,
A sacred space where time can bend.

Through silken veils, we twirl and glide,
In every glance, we can't divide.
With laughter bright, and shadows deep,
In this dance, our spirits leap.

So take my hand, let's venture forth,
In this dance of hidden worth.
With every step, we'll break the mold,
In depths uncharted, we'll be bold.

The Veil Less Tread

Through misty paths we tread with care,
Beneath the stars, our dreams to share.
With whispered winds, the night entreats,
A world awakes as silence greets.

In shadows deep, our secrets lie,
In every corner, echoes sigh.
The heart feels free, the spirit bold,
As ancient tales of hope unfold.

With every step, a truth we seek,
In courage found, our voices speak.
The veil between, a fragile thread,
A journey new, less fear, less dread.

Awake the dawn, a chance to rise,
With open hearts, we claim the skies.
Each footfall writes a destiny,
In the boundless realm, we wander free.

And as we roam, our souls connect,
In nature's arms, we can reflect.
A path less tread, so lives entwined,
Reveal the light we seek to find.

Listen to the Stillness

In quiet moments, hearts will hear,
The whispers soft, so crystal clear.
With gentle breath, the world awakes,
In silent prayer, the spirit shakes.

The solitude of dusk does blend,
With peace that wraps, our souls to mend.
In stillness held, a truth unveiled,
Where joy and sorrow both have sailed.

The stars above, they twinkle bright,
In harmony with coming night.
A hush of thoughts, the mind will cease,
And in that pause, we find our peace.

Embrace the calm, don't rush away,
For in the stillness, dreams may play.
The world outside can wait, it's true,
In silence found, we start anew.

So listen close, let thoughts be few,
In gentle grace, life's essence grew.
Each heartbeat echoes in the night,
A symphony of pure delight.

Nature's Subtle Messages

In every leaf, a story breathes,
Each rustling voice, the heart perceives.
A gentle sway, the branches' song,
In nature's arms, we all belong.

The morning dew, a sparkling gem,
Reflecting light from realms within.
In whispers sweet, the breeze will bring,
A language soft, of life in spring.

The mountains stand, their wisdom vast,
With ancient roots, they hold the past.
In every stream, a truth flows free,
The universe speaks endlessly.

With open eyes, we sense the flow,
In every moment, learn and grow.
A flower's bloom, a silent cheer,
The subtle signs that draw us near.

Listen closely, heed the sound,
Of nature's voice in all around.
In every stone, in every tree,
The messages of peace shall be.

Tints of Authentic Revelation

In colors bold, the canvas shines,
With every stroke, the heart aligns.
The hues of truth, so warm, so bright,
In every shadow lies the light.

Through grays and blues, the pain reveals,
A palette rich, the spirit heals.
The golden rays, a gentle kiss,
Awaken dreams we can't dismiss.

Each shade an echo, whispers strong,
In every note, we learn the song.
A splash of red, of love and fire,
In vivid tones, our souls conspire.

With every turn, the world transforms,
A dance of life, a storm that warms.
Authentic shades enrich our view,
In tints of dreams, let's rise anew.

So paint your heart with every breath,
In strokes of joy, defying death.
The canvas waits, as thoughts unfold,
A story bright, a truth retold.

The Softest Confessions

Whispers dance upon the air,
Words that flutter, light as care.
Secrets tucked in shadows deep,
In quiet moments, silence keeps.

A fragile truth, so hard to find,
Yet in the soul, it's intertwined.
The heart reveals what lips won't say,
In tender light, it finds its way.

Fingers trace the lines of fate,
A tapestry of love, innate.
Soft confessions beneath the moon,
In dusk's embrace, they find their tune.

Echoes linger in the night,
Softly glowing, pure delight.
Each admission, a gentle sigh,
Under stars, our dreams can fly.

So listen close, as feelings bloom,
In hushed tones, dispelling gloom.
The softest confessions we hold dear,
In quiet corners, hearts draw near.

Tapestry of Unvoiced Dreams

In the dusk, dreams start to weave,
Threads of hope that we believe.
Colors blend in shadows' play,
Unvoiced wishes find their way.

Stitched in silence, desires grow,
Patterns bloom, and visions flow.
Each moment sown with tender care,
A tapestry, both rare and fair.

Fingers glide on fabric fine,
Stories waiting for the sign.
Whispers echo, soft and clear,
In every stitch, our dreams appear.

Memories rise like morning's light,
Unspooled tales take graceful flight.
Embroidered dreams our hearts unite,
In woven threads, we find our sight.

Beneath the stars, our hopes ignite,
We dare to dream beyond the night.
A tapestry, both bold and bright,
Holding secrets, love's true light.

Breath of Insight

In silence, wisdom starts to bloom,
A breath held tight, dispelling gloom.
Through gentle winds, ideas flow,
In the stillness, minds will grow.

A whisper shifts the sands of time,
Quiet thoughts begin to rhyme.
Moments pause, then rush away,
In that hush, insights play.

Feel the pulse of truth within,
Guiding light through where we've been.
Each inhalation brings us near,
To thoughts we hold, yet seldom hear.

The dawn reveals each hidden thought,
In breathless calm, connections sought.
In stillness, paths of light align,
With every breath, our hearts entwine.

So breathe in deep, let knowledge rise,
Awaken dreams under vast skies.
A breath of insight, soft and pure,
In every pause, we're meant to soar.

Faint Sounds of Honesty

In the echoes, truth resides,
Faint sounds where honesty abides.
A gentle sigh, a whispered word,
In fragile moments, hearts are heard.

Through shadows deep, a voice will break,
Softly speaking, for courage's sake.
Honesty wrapped in tender hues,
A quiet strength we dare to choose.

The rhythm of the heart reveals,
The simple truths that love conceals.
In every pause, a longing finds,
The faintest sounds of open minds.

Each confession, a flaring spark,
Illuminating paths so dark.
With gentle grace, we lift the veil,
In whispered tones, we will not fail.

For honesty, though soft and meek,
Is strength in what it dares to speak.
With courage, we embrace the sound,
In faint whispers, truth is found.

Shadows of the Heart

In whispers dim, the shadows play,
They dance around, then fade away.
A tender hope, a silent plea,
Lost in the echoes, just you and me.

Through corridors of love we roam,
Each heartbeat leads us closer home.
With every dusk, new dreams ignite,
In shadows deep, we find our light.

The past, a ghost that lingers near,
Yet in this dusk, I hold you dear.
Together we embrace the night,
Where shadows merge to share our plight.

A gentle touch, a fleeting glance,
Within the dark, we find romance.
With echoes soft and breaths combined,
Our hearts entwined, forever blind.

So let us walk through twilight's door,
Where shadows linger, evermore.
In every breath, our souls align,
In shadows deep, your heart is mine.

The Unspoken Journey

Across the hills where silence sings,
A journey starts with unseen wings.
In quiet steps, we trace the lines,
Of dreams that whisper, love defines.

Through winding paths, the unknown calls,
In every rise, a shadow falls.
The road ahead, a mystic fate,
In unvoiced truths, we navigate.

With every mile, a story grows,
In hidden tales, the spirit flows.
We wander far, yet close we stand,
In unspoken words, we understand.

Beware the doubts that cloud the skies,
For in the dark, our guidance lies.
Step boldly forth, with hearts ablaze,
The unspoken path, a sacred maze.

Together through the winds we glide,
In trust we find our souls reside.
The journey ends, but love won't part,
Forever etched, in every heart.

Hints of Clarity

In twilight's glow, the world is clear,
A moment paused, all thoughts draw near.
With every breath, the truth unveils,
In gentle whispers, clarity sails.

As colors blend and shadows fade,
In quiet moments, bright truths parade.
Echoes of doubt dissolve like sand,
With hints of light, we take a stand.

The heart learns well from time's soft grace,
In every smile, we find our place.
Through tangled paths and storms that rage,
This journey leads us to the page.

For in the stillness, wisdom blooms,
In subtle signs, the spirit looms.
We sift through dreams, both near and far,
To find our strength, to be a star.

So take the leap, embrace the now,
With hints of clarity, we vow.
Together we'll chase the paths we seek,
In each heart's whisper, love will speak.

Lullabies of Reality

In shadows low, where dreams reside,
A lullaby sings, with hope as guide.
It tugs at hearts, a gentle sway,
In whispers soft, it finds a way.

The world outside may seem unkind,
Yet in these verses, peace we find.
With every note, the soul takes flight,
In lullabies, we chase the night.

Each melody, a story spun,
Of battles fought and victory won.
Through trials faced, we hold on tight,
To lullabies that warm the night.

So let the rhythms soothe the mind,
In every ebb, a love refined.
The heart's embrace, a tender sound,
In lullabies of love, we're bound.

With every breath, let peace unfold,
In lullabies, the truth is told.
Together we find what dreams can be,
In reality's arms, you're here with me.

Unraveled Mysteries

In shadows deep, a tale untold,
Whispers dance where secrets unfold.
Through tangled roots, the truth does creep,
An ancient dream, a timeless leap.

With every twist, a heart beats raw,
Unveiling depths, revealing flaw.
Each clue a step, a map to trace,
The eyes awake to time and space.

Beneath the stars, the questions roam,
In hidden paths, we find our home.
With every sigh, we find our way,
Unraveled threads of night and day.

In silent rooms, the echoes ring,
Ghosts of thought, the song they sing.
Through open doors, the light shall spill,
Unraveled truths and quiet will.

The Quiet Call of Authenticity

In silent whispers, truth begins,
A gentle pull that draws us in.
Amidst the noise of fleeting trends,
The heart's soft voice forever blends.

With courage found in tender grace,
We lift the mask, reveal our face.
In every flaw, a story shines,
Authenticity, like vintage wines.

Through crowded rooms, we walk our path,
Embracing joy, releasing wrath.
The quiet call, a steadfast guide,
In truth, we stand, and there abide.

Through trials faced and lessons learned,
The essence of our souls discerned.
For in the depths, we truly find,
The courage birthed when hearts unwind.

Sunbeams through the Fog

When morning breaks, the shadows gleam,
Sunbeams cut through the misty dream.
A golden touch on water's skin,
Awakening the world within.

The fog wraps tight, a soft embrace,
Yet warmth intrudes to leave its trace.
A dance of light, the whispers soft,
In gentle rays, our spirits loft.

Each golden shard, a promise made,
A subtle path where fears do fade.
Through veils of gray, the colors hum,
Inviting all, the light will come.

With every step, the fog recedes,
Revealing blooms and sprouting seeds.
In harmony, the light will stay,
As hearts embrace the brand new day.

Hidden Narratives

In pages worn, the stories lie,
Silent witnesses to the sky.
Each word a brush, each line a stroke,
Painting thoughts that softly spoke.

Beneath the surface, currents flow,
Whispers weaving tales of woe.
In laughter shared and tears that fall,
We find the truth within it all.

From shadows cast, a voice will rise,
Revealing dreams, dispelling lies.
In every heart, a chapter waits,
The hidden paths that love creates.

Through ink and time, the moments blend,
Each pulse a thread that never ends.
Together bound, our stories blend,
In hidden tales, we find our friends.

The Language of Silence

In shadows deep, a whisper flows,
Unspoken thoughts, where stillness grows.
A gentle pause, the heart's embrace,
In silence, there's a sacred space.

Words unneeded, feelings known,
In quietude, true selves are shown.
The hush holds dreams we dare not share,
In silence, we find solace rare.

Echoes linger, thoughts entwined,
In quiet whispers, we unwind.
The language formed from breathless sighs,
In silent realms, our spirits rise.

Yet from the stillness, voices soar,
Transforming silence into more.
Each muted note, a song refined,
In the language of silence, we find.

So let us cherish each soft sigh,
In the depths where secrets lie.
For in the pauses, life confides,
The language of silence abides.

Soft Sounds of Awareness

A rustle here, a whisper there,
Awakening thoughts, floating in air.
The soft sounds call, a gentle tease,
Inviting minds to rest and breathe.

The drip of rain, the fluttering leaf,
In each small sound, we find relief.
A world alive with subtle cues,
Each note a spark, our minds enthuse.

In fleeting moments, we become aware,
Of soft vibrations that fill the air.
The peace it brings, a seasoned balm,
In soft sounds, we find our calm.

Distant laughter, a child's delight,
The chirp of birds at morning light.
In sounds of nature, truth rings clear,
In every note, our hearts draw near.

So let us listen, truly hear,
The soft sounds whispering near.
Awareness blooms in quiet space,
In each soft sound, we find our place.

Truths Between the Lines

In every tale, a truth concealed,
Between the lines, fate's revealed.
A dance of shadows, hints of light,
In hidden realms, we seek the bright.

The words may twist, the meaning change,
Yet in our hearts, we rearrange.
To grasp the essence, we must dig,
For truths emerge, both slight and big.

What's left unspoken, often screams,
In subtle ways, we weave our dreams.
The silence speaks, the gaps define,
The stories old, the ties that bind.

Trace your fingers on the page,
Feel the wisdom, feel the age.
In every pause, a thought aligns,
We find the truths between the lines.

So read with care, with heart and mind,
For in the margins, we all find.
A treasure trove of thoughts divine,
The hidden truths between the lines.

The Gentle Rustle of Discovery

As leaves unfold, a secret shared,
The gentle sound, a world prepared.
In rustling whispers, journeys start,
Each turn, a new beat of the heart.

With footsteps soft, we wander through,
Each rustle hints at wonders new.
Unseen paths of light and shade,
In gentle rustles, dreams are laid.

The breeze carries tales of old,
In each soft rustle, stories told.
Awakening senses, spirits soar,
In discovery, we crave for more.

What lies beneath the surface sheen?
A marvel waiting to be seen.
The gentle rustle guides our way,
In quiet prompts, we find our play.

So step with care, let curiosity lead,
In rustling leaves, there's magic freed.
In every sound, a gift awaits,
The gentle rustle of discovery states.

Tangles of Perception

In shadows cast by thoughts so deep,
We wander through the paths we keep.
Each twist and turn, a new reveal,
Yet truth remains a fragile deal.

Through lenses clear, or hazed with doubt,
We sift through dreams, what's in and out.
Perceptions shift, like sands at sea,
What's yours is not what's meant for me.

In every glance, a different tale,
Some voices linger, others pale.
The tapestry of mind unfurls,
A maze of thoughts, a dance of whirls.

Expectations shape what we may find,
As fleeting moments redefine.
Each judgment casts a lasting line,
In tangled thoughts, our fates entwine.

So tread with care on this fine thread,
Each word you speak, from what is said.
For in this web of what we see,
The heart holds truths yet to be free.

Whispers in the Wind

In quiet times, the breezes sigh,
They tell of dreams that dare to fly.
Among the trees, whispers abound,
Secrets of nature softly found.

With every gust, stories unfold,
Of ancient paths and tales retold.
The wind's embrace, a tender kiss,
Carries with it a sense of bliss.

Through meadows wide, and valleys low,
The whispers dance, a constant flow.
They brush our skin, a fleeting touch,
A promise held, it means so much.

In twilight's glow, they gently weave,
A fabric rich, we can believe.
These whispers shared, a friend to seek,
In silence breaks, they softly speak.

So let the wind guide where you go,
In every breath, let wisdom grow.
For whispers heard in nature's breath,
Bring life anew, beyond all death.

Hidden Messages in the Breeze

The air is thick with tales untold,
In subtle signs, the brave unfold.
Beneath the surface, whispers dwell,
Messages wrapped, a magic spell.

As leaves flutter, hearts do cringe,
In every breeze, a cracking hinge.
Unraveling thoughts, we stand in awe,
What seems a flaw could be a law.

Each rustling leaf, a code we seek,
The essence of what nature speaks.
With an open heart, we dive inside,
In hidden truths, we cannot hide.

For in this dance of light and shade,
The universe has gently laid.
A fabric rich with insight pure,
In every breeze, we can endure.

So heed the signs, let intuition lead,
In simple whispers, plant the seed.
For hidden messages, softly blessed,
In nature's weave, our souls can rest.

Luminescent Secrets

In twilight's glow, secrets ignite,
Soft sparkles dance in fading light.
Hidden gems in shadows bloom,
Illuminating every room.

Through darkness deep, a shimmer calls,
In whispered dreams, where magic falls.
The luminescence, a guiding star,
Revealing wonders, near and far.

These secrets held within our gaze,
Illuminate the often-maze.
With open eyes, we seek to find,
The brilliance in the heart and mind.

A touch of light, a gentle grace,
In moments still, we find our place.
As each flicker tells a tale,
Of love and loss, our spirits sail.

So treasure the glow, let it abide,
For in each secret, dreams reside.
Enchanted realms where shadows play,
Shine in our hearts, forever stay.

Secrets in the Silence

In shadows cast by fading light,
Whispers dance and take their flight.
Hidden truths in muted tones,
Lingering soft like ancient bones.

Ghostly echoes fill the air,
Where silence wraps, secrets ensnare.
A heartbeat missed, a sigh contained,
In quiet corners, dreams are gained.

The stillness hides what time forgets,
And in the hush, our souls are met.
Each thought a ripple, softly spun,
In silence deep, we come undone.

Listen close, the night implores,
For all it hides behind locked doors.
In every pause, life's hopes emerge,
Inside the silence, dreams converge.

So seek the secrets, hold them tight,
In shadows deep, find your light.
For in the stillness, truth can gleam,
Revealing paths in whispers, dream.

Echoes of the Unseen

Beneath the skin, a pulse of sound,
A world alive in silence found.
Where shadows play and vision fades,
The unseen dances, fear evades.

In corners dark, where echoes lie,
Patterns weave and spirits sigh.
Every heartbeat, every breath,
Concealing life, embracing death.

Whispers flow through hidden seams,
Reality drifts on fragmented dreams.
Glimmers of truth, just out of sight,
In the unseen, sparks the light.

Listen closely, heed the call,
For in the quiet, we stand tall.
Embrace the shadows, let them speak,
In echoes of the unseen, we seek.

As time slips by, we're intertwined,
With all that's lost and all enshrined.
In silent screams, find your release,
In echoes of the unseen, find peace.

Veils of Revelation

Behind the veil, truths lie concealed,
Mysteries grasped, yet never revealed.
Layers thick with tales untold,
Underneath, the world is bold.

A gentle pull, the fabric frays,
Revealing shadows of brighter days.
What once was lost, now reborn,
In veils of revelation, hearts are worn.

Each fold a story, each tear a cry,
Whispers linger, as moments fly.
Searching for light in every seam,
In veils we find the hidden dream.

With every touch, new visions bloom,
Life unfolds and dispels the gloom.
Courage found in delicate grace,
As we unveil this sacred space.

In thinnest layers, wisdom flows,
Among the veils, the spirit grows.
Eager to see what's kept inside,
In veils of revelation, we abide.

Murmurs Beneath the Surface

Rippling waters softly sway,
Murmurs whisper, night and day.
Beneath the calm, a storm may brew,
Hidden depths, both old and new.

In silence wrought with gentle grace,
Voices echo, find their place.
Look closer now, what lies beneath,
In every pulse, in every breath.

Secrets buried in soft terrain,
Murmurs float like gentle rain.
A tapestry of life we weave,
In every sigh, we do believe.

The surface glimmers, worlds collide,
What flows within we cannot hide.
Between the lines, the truth takes form,
In murmurs deep, our spirits warm.

So take a breath and dive right in,
To seek the wealth that lies within.
For in the depths, we find our worth,
In murmurs beneath the surface, rebirth.